S0-BZI-939

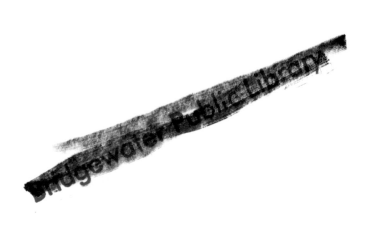
Bridgewater Public Library

CountryMusic ★ Stars
BRAD PAISLEY

By Therese Shea

Gareth Stevens
Publishing

Please visit our Web site, www.garethstevens.com. For a free color catalog of all our high-quality books, call toll free 1-800-542-2595 or fax 1-877-542-2596.

Library of Congress Cataloging-in-Publication Data

Shea, Therese.
 Brad Paisley / Therese Shea.
   p. cm. — (Country music stars)
 Includes index.
 ISBN 978-1-4339-3930-3 (pbk.)
 ISBN 978-1-4339-3931-0 (6-pack)
 ISBN 978-1-4339-3929-7 (library binding)
 1. Paisley, Brad—Juvenile literature. 2. Country musicians—United States—
Biography—Juvenile literature. I. Title.
 ML3930.P225S44 2011
 782.421642092—dc22

 [B]
                                 2010000413

First Edition

Published in 2011 by
Gareth Stevens Publishing
111 East 14th Street, Suite 349
New York, NY 10003

Copyright © 2011 Gareth Stevens Publishing

Designer: Haley W. Harasymiw
Editor: Therese Shea

Photo credits: Cover background Shutterstock.com; cover (Brad Paisley) Larry Busacca/
Getty Images; p. 5 Rusty Russell/Getty Images; p. 7 Amanda Edwards/Getty Images;
pp. 9, 17 Kevin Winter/Getty Images; pp. 11, 13, 23, 25 Rick Diamond/Getty Images;
p. 15 Michael Caulfield/Getty Images; p. 19 Billy Kingsley/Getty Images; p. 21 Vince
Bucci/Getty Images; p. 27 Ronald C. Modra/Sports Imagery/Getty Images; p. 29
Frederick Breedon/Getty Images.

All rights reserved. No part of this book may be reproduced in any form without
permission in writing from the publisher, except by a reviewer.

Printed in the United States of America

CPSIA compliance information: Batch #CS10GS: For further information contact Gareth Stevens, New York, New York at 1-800-542-2595.

CONTENTS

ONE OF THE GREATS

Brad Paisley is one of the best country music singers today. He plays guitar and writes music, too.

STARTING OUT

Brad was born on October 28, 1972. He lived in a town called Glen Dale in West Virginia.

Brad's grandfather gave him a guitar when he was 8 years old. He taught Brad to play, too.

9

When he was 12, Brad played in his first band. It was called the C-Notes.

In 1984, a radio station asked Brad to play his music on a show. He continued to play on the radio show for several years.

BRAD'S BIG BREAK

Brad went to a college in Nashville, Tennessee. He met many people who helped him with his music.

Brad began working for a record company. He wrote songs for other people to sing. He wrote songs for himself, too.

17

Brad's first album came out in 1999. It was called *Who Needs Pictures*. In 2000, Brad was given awards for being the best new artist.

19

Brad has won several Grammys, too. However, he says he would love to play football for the Cleveland Browns!

MUSICAL FRIENDS

Brad sings with other country music stars. He has sung with Carrie Underwood.

Carrie Underwood

23

Brad makes music videos, too. Taylor Swift was in a music video for his song "Online."

Taylor Swift

MUSIC AND FAMILY

Brad writes music about life and even fishing! His music makes people laugh and cry.

Brad has a family. His wife, Kimberly, is an actress. They have two sons named William Huckleberry and Jasper Warren.

Kimberly Williams-Paisley

29

TIMELINE

1972   Brad is born in Glen Dale, West Virginia.

1980   Brad learns to play the guitar.

1984   Brad begins to play on the radio.

1999   Brad's first album comes out.

2000   Brad is given awards for best new artist.

2008   Brad wins his first Grammy.

FOR MORE INFORMATION

Books:

Bertholf, Bret. *The Long Gone Lonesome History of Country Music.* New York, NY: Little, Brown and Company, 2007.

Lindeen, Mary. *Cool Country Music: Create & Appreciate What Makes Music Great!* Edina, MN: ABDO Publishing, 2008.

Web Sites:

Brad Paisley: Official Site
bradpaisley.musiccitynetworks.com/

CMT.com: Brad Paisley Biography
www.cmt.com/artists/az/paisley_brad/bio.jhtml

Publisher's note to educators and parents: Our editors have carefully reviewed these Web sites to ensure that they are suitable for students. Many Web sites change frequently, however, and we cannot guarantee that a site's future contents will continue to meet our high standards of quality and educational value. Be advised that students should be closely supervised whenever they access the Internet.

GLOSSARY

award: a prize given to someone for doing something well

college: a school after high school

Grammy: an award given to someone for their music

record company: a business that produces and sells music

video: a short movie that goes along with a song

INDEX